Thinking and Doing

MOSHE FELDENKRAIS

Forewords by Moti Nativ and Professor Hugo Bergman
Preface by Professors Hans and Shulamit Kreitler
Translation from Hebrew into English by Reuven Ofir

Genesis II Publishing
Longmont, Colorado
AchievingExcellence.com

Feldenkrais, Moshe, 1904 – 1984.

The Practice of Autosuggestion by the method of Émile Coué / by Moshe
Feldenkrais © 1929, 1977 now the Israeli *Feldenkrais* Guild and the Silice
Family, portions gratefully used by their permission.

New foreword and archival photographs by Moti Nativ.

For information contact Genesis II Publishing, Inc.

Feldenkrais®, *Feldenkrais Method*®,
Functional Integration®, and *Awareness Through Movement*®,
are Service marks of The *Feldenkrais* Guild®

Published by Genesis II Publishing, Inc.
P.O. Box 2615, Longmont, CO 80502
www.AchievingExcellence.com

Printed in the United States of America
ISBN: 978-1-884605-26-0
CIP: 2013949050

As addressed within Coué's work and in Feldenkrais's commentary, one must begin by understanding that fundamentally in matters of self-control and self-direction Imagination trumps Will. By locating the self-image as a product of self-imaging we can bypass notions of the unconscious and discern how Feldenkrais acquired one of the key pillars of his life's work.

If, as Moshe Feldenkrais held, the unconscious is not unconscious, how did he get to that position? First, using Coué's work, he immersed himself in a practical course of study on how to use the unconscious to make one's life better. Along the way he realized that the unconscious is not a thing but a process with constraints that are amenable to utilization. As such, what does that mean for notions of the sub-conscious, consciousness itself and the vast, vague domain of so-called altered states of consciousness? If we view those terms as territorial maps then the maps should correspond to their respective territories. Feldenkrais realized that the terms were less than helpful ad hoc human inventions having little pragmatic value. The processes they would map, viewed from Feldenkrais's perspective of awareness, require a radically different approach.

—Dennis Leri, *Feldenkrais®* Trainer

Contents

Introduction

The commentary by Moshe Feldenkrais, the foreword by Professor Hugo Bergman and the preface by Professors Hans and Shulamit Kreitler were translated from Hebrew into English by Reuven Ofir.

In 1929 Moshe Feldenkrais published his Hebrew translation of the book *The Practice of Autosuggestion by the Method of Émile Coué*, originally published in English by C. Harry Brooks.[1] Professor Hugo Bergman, first rector of the Hebrew University in Jerusalem, wrote the foreword and Moshe wrote some twenty-six pages of commentary. Moshe's book was reissued in 1977, with the addition of a preface by Professor Hans Kreitler, who headed the Department of Behavioral Sciences at Tel Aviv University, and Shulamit Kreitler, Associate Professor, who lectured in the Department of Psychology at Tel Aviv University. At the invitation of Professor Kreitler, Dr. Feldenkrais delivered a series of lectures at the university.

Acknowledgements

I offer my heartfelt thanks to the Feldenkrais and Silice families for their support and for granting permission for the book to be translated and published, and the great help provided by the president of the Israeli Guild, Ramona Dekel, as she shepherded this project through the legal intricacies culminating in getting all concerned parties to sign the necessary contracts and get the ball rolling. My thanks are offered to Doron Tadmor for assisting me

i

in my initial faltering steps in this work, and to Dennis Leri for his encouragement. To Moti Nativ I owe thanks for his unrelenting demands to stay true to the spirit and soul of Moshe's writings, and for providing such a valuable postscript of his own to this work, in which he illuminates the past and provides context for the period in Moshe's life during which he translated and wrote his commentary to C. Harry Brooks' work on Emile Coué's work.

I am grateful to Eva Laser for lovingly frowning at me and telling me I could do better, after I wrote the first and second drafts. Lastly, I offer my sincere thanks to Al Wadleigh for his generous contribution in bringing this little pamphlet to publication.

Translator's note

In a learned treatise, the Roman grammarian Varro pointed out that he had discovered two hundred twenty-eight distinct meanings for the word "good." The Italian proverb *"traduttorre, tradittore"* ("The translator is a betrayer"), by Clyde Kluckhohn[2], is all too correct. In this translation I have done my best to betray the author as little as possible. I hope I will be forgiven for any lapses.

Moshe worked on translating Brooks' work into Hebrew some eighty-five years ago when he was in his twenties. Given the context of the times in terms of his use of Hebrew, Biblical references, and metaphors, as well as his references to people who may have faded from the collective memory, I have taken the liberty of providing meta comments and sources with the aim of offering some additional background, context, and clarity. These comments and sources are in the form of endnotes.

> —Reuven (Robbie) Ofir, Ph.d, P.T., *Feldenkrais* Trainer and former supervisor of Physical Therapy at NYU Medical Center Rusk Rehabilitation Institute, Miami Beach, Florida

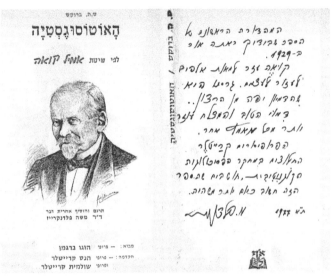

The following is a translation by Reuven Ofir of the hand-written note Feldenkrais made on a copy of his 1977 publication of *Autosuggestion*.

The first edition of the book you are holding saw light in 1929.

Coué helped hundreds of thousands help themselves.

His idea is that imagination is more important than will-power. Imagining the good and the successful helps more than any other striving.

The Kreitler professors, pioneers in cognitive research, believe this book is more important these days than in the past.

—M. Feldenkrais, Tel Aviv, Israel, 1977

Foreword

You have witnessed me in my distress, and this here is the beginning of my potency.
—Moshe Feldenkrais

Autosuggestion was published at the end of 1929. At the time, it was defined as a translation of the book written by C. H. Brooks, but reading it many years after it was published singles out the uniqueness of the young translator. Moshe Feldenkrais not only translated the book, but composed and added his own observations in the two chapters you are about to read.

Looking back, we can clearly see that at that time Moshe reached a significant milestone in his life that combined his diverse activities and interests into the path that henceforth would lead him to develop his method, *Awareness Through Movement*®.

A comprehensive reference to the contents of the book will not be complete, in my opinion, without pointing out important details of Moshe's life at that chapter, the progression of which reached its peak with the translation of the book *Autosuggestion*.

The chapter begins in 1918 with the voyage of fourteen year-old Moshe to Palestine, landing in 1919 at the port of Jaffa. It ends in 1930 with Moshe leaving for France and starting his next chapter. In the Israeli history books these were the years of the third and fourth *Aliyah*, or ascension, which refers to the waves of Jewish immigration to Palestine during the years 1919 – 1924 and 1925 – 1931.

Young Moshe lived the life of the pioneers. He and his friends did hard manual labor building houses in Tel Aviv by day and danced and had meetings in the evening. They guarded through the night what they had built during the day.

Photo courtesy of the Haganna Archives.

In the picture above from 1920, Moshe stands (bare headed, on the upper left side of the picture) with his friends from the Baranovitch group (his home town, today in Belarus), with whom he worked, danced, and guarded.

The life Moshe led at the time revealed his mental flexibility, which indeed guided him later in his life, but he mainly stood out as a survivor and a fighter. This aspect of his character enabled him to withstand many hardships and direct them into development and progress.

I found a story demonstrating Moshe's character in a book from 1964 by Yehuda Erez called *The Third Aliya* where he quotes the testimony of Avigdor Grinshpan, "Notes of a teacher turned laborer", Tel Aviv, 1920:

> My teacher on the site was a former pupil of mine named Moshe Feldenkrais. He was a young boy, around sixteen years old, broad shouldered and sturdy as an oak. Feldenkrais assigned me the task of climbing up to the second story of the building with him carrying pallets full of cement and heavy stones. Feldenkrais paid no attention to my groans and urged me to climb. "Make an effort, Grinshpan" he said flatteringly. "Pay no attention to the suffering: The Torah drains your strength, not the work. The work makes life sweet."
>
> When I entreated him not to hurry so, he answered me, "You are my spiritual teacher, and I listen to you and obey you. I, however, am your material teacher and therefore you must obey me! You will eventually see that I am right."

An important landmark at that time was the establishing of the Haganna, or defense organization, in 1920. Moshe joined the Haganna and took part in brutal street fights defending Tel Aviv neighborhoods against attackers. From historical records, we learn of numerous casualties among these defenders. Moshe decided there was urgent need of creating a self defense method to assist his friends in the Haganna and indeed, with interesting timing, at the same time as his work on *Autosuggestion* he investigated and developed his own strategy for self defense.

So, towards the end of 1930, a few months after the publication of *Autosuggestion*, he published another book, *Jiu-Jitsu and Self-Defense*. This was the first Isreali self-defense book. The book, born out of his experiences in the bloody street brawls of Tel Aviv, was linked to a large extent with his insight from *Autosuggestion*. Today we also know that this book had an important part in Moshe's very significant meeting with Jigoro Kano, the founder of Judo.

The photo and the final process of the self-defense book were done in hurry. The photo was taken on October 10, 1930, and the book was printed within few days after. Moshe signed a few copies for close friends and left for France for his next life chapter. As Moshe told Dennis Leri, one of his first American students, in the interview, during the San Francisco training in 1977: "The British, if the book fell into their hands and they knew that I wrote it, they would probably arrest me and ask me who the leaders of the Haganah were and so on. So the day the book was published, I was in France."

Photo taken in studio Plastica, Alenby St., Tel Aviv. Courtesy of Moti Nativ's private collection.

It can be said without hesitation that Moshe by now contained within him all the ingredients required for developing the *Feldenkrais Method*®.

His qualifications in mathematics and physics as student and teacher were already proven. He had delved deeply into the field of psychology, and added to it his knowledge from his studies of

Moshe's note and signature to a friend on the back of his portrait.

Autosuggestion. He trained himself in martial arts and taught his friends as well. In addition, he was already carrying perhaps the most recognized component in his development: his severely injured left knee caused during a game of soccer, his favorite sport. In time, it was learning to function with this knee that influenced the development of his method.

Moshe had an inherent genius and strong desire to explore deeply any subject matter that came across his way—qualities already evident when still at Herzliya high school from which he graduated with honors. This, combined with his meeting with people who became inscribed in the history of Israel, shaped his world view and would influence him all his life. Among these figures, Professor Hugo Bergman was especially important for Moshe. He deeply appreciated him, kept in constant contact, and used to share his life events with him.

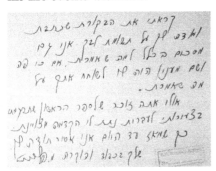

Photo of this part of the letter to Bergman. Courtesy of the Department of Archives, the National Library of Israel.

After the publication of the French translation of his self-defense book he sent Bergman a copy along with a long letter. He described his meetings with Professor Jigoro Kano and his professional relations with him. He spoke with enthusiasm about Judo and of the appreciation he received from Kano.

In 1967 he gave Professor Bergman a copy of his book, *Improving Abilities (Awareness Through Movement)* and received his remarks. Moshe responded with a letter ending with words of thanks: "You may recall that for the first book I translated as a young man to Hebrew, you wrote an excellent foreword, since then I have been very grateful to you."

Let me now touch upon a number of aspects directly related to the book *Autosuggestion*. First, we have to bear in mind that Moshe wrote in what is now considered archaic Hebrew and translating his words to any other language detracts from the rhythm and musicality of the original writing.

I. The Personal Aspect

During the period in which he wrote, Moshe experienced the joys of youth but also suffered from poverty and illness. Publication of his book was in Moshe's mind the beginning of better days. He expressed his feelings in the dedication he wrote on the first edition copy he gave to the Rubinstein family (the family of his future wife, Yona). Moshe wrote: "You have witnessed me in my distress, and this here is the beginning of my potency."

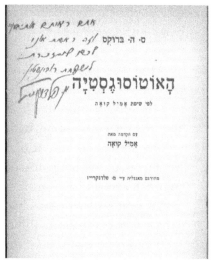

Autosuggestion remained for many years to come a reference point for Moshe as he continued to develop his work. He mentioned Coué in various aspects in his later publications, among them his two books, *Body and Mature Behavior* (1947), and *Improving Abilities* (1967). These two books are considered milestones in the development of the *Feldenkrais Method*.

Book Cover of *Autosuggestion* with dedication courtesy of Moti's friend Ilan Jacobson.

Significant evidence for his strong connection to *Autosuggestion* is found in his efforts to re-publish the book in 1977, sweeping up his friends Hans and Shulamit Kreitler, professors of psychology, with his enthusiasm for Coué.

Moshe's acquaintance with Professor Hans Kreitler started in the 1960s. Hans, head of the Faculty of Psychology at Tel Aviv University, invited Moshe to lecture and gave him a teaching post from 1965-1966. They became friends and Moshe was a frequent guest in the Kreitlers' home.

Professor Shulamit Kreitler was, and still is, a lecturer at the School of Psychological Science at Tel Aviv University. She admires Moshe and his method and even applied principles of the *Feldenkrais Method* in her work treating people suffering from chronic pain. For a while she participated in his *Awareness Through Movement* lessons at Alexander Yanai and later received *Functional Integration*® lessons from him.

In our meetings, Shulamit told me how she used to watch Hans and Moshe engaged in intense discussions with the term "body and mind" repeated often like a mantra. She said to me, "Moshe was a fighter."

At her request, I will tell of her first and last meetings with Moshe.

At their first meeting, so she told me, he put his Judo book in front of her and declared: "I am a martial artist."

She was very moved when she told me of their last meeting. Moshe was in the hospital on his deathbed, already cut off from his surroundings. Shulamit sat next to him on the bed and led his hand to her back. Suddenly she felt Moshe passing his finger, clearly and precisely, on the apex of the S curve of the scoliosis which he had treated in her back. That moment, she said, moved her still.

One additional point from the personal aspect, which can also belong to the professional one, is the link Moshe made between prayer and autosuggestion. The pioneering Jewish environment in Tel Aviv was mainly secular, but it seemed Moshe was still influenced by the orthodox education from his childhood. In his writings he expounded on the meaning of prayer as autosuggestion, bringing in examples from Rabbinical quotations as further evidence for its power.

II. The Professional Aspect

I will point out two relevant issues, and I am certain the readers will discern others. The first is Moshe's clarifications of concepts and insights from *Autosuggestion* which, in the future, were to appear as basic elements of *Awareness Through Movement*.

The second is Moshe's application of the functional use of the unconscious in self-preservation, a principle which served him in efficient teaching of self-defense techniques.

Moshe writes about the three basic characteristics of autosuggestion in creating the imagined movement patterns leading to action. When we do that, we can implement the action without mental interference brought by the urge to succeed as a result of doubts and lack of self-confidence. The pleasure and ease of functioning accompanied by positive associations will then increase our motivation to act as well as elevating our vital potency.

Moshe expressed himself wisely about the difficulty of applying effective action when hampered by willpower in his book, *The Potent Self* (p. 193): "Hurry and effort are not substitute for skill—they always indicate the presence of doubt of one's own ability to cope with the situation. The motivation to succeed is, in such cases, stronger than the motivation to act."

In his conclusion to the contribution of imaging a movement in the mind prior to its enactment, Moshe also responds to the topic he raised in his opening remarks. In fact, he points the way to perfecting the healthy individual by elevating his inherent capabilities as a means of achieving superior results. Image of action and perfecting abilities are without doubt basic principles of *Awareness*

Through Movement and it is here where we recognize the first clear link to the future *Feldenkrais Method*.

Integrating the conscious with the unconscious

Coincidentally, as Moshe was translating Brooks' *Autosuggestion*, he was investigating the reasons for the bitter outcomes of the recent street fights in which many of his friends were injured or killed. He was concerned by the inefficiency of the Haganna members in battles despite their success in Jiu-Jitsu trainings. His conclusion from the attacks and the defensive responses was that people react instinctively against surprise attacks, reverting to an unconscious reaction which protects vital parts of the body, even if they have no knowledge of anatomy.

In the concluding chapters of *Autosuggestion,* Moshe describes from experience a man bending forward in response to a threat in order to protect his solar plexus, or a man with no previous martial art skills shielding his head with his hands when a stick is waved towards it. He defines the unconscious as an immense hidden treasure of knowledge and memories.

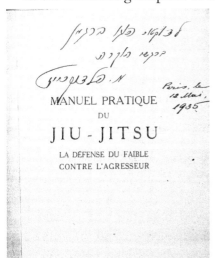

This is the copy of Manuel Pratique du Jiu-Jitsu that Moshe dedicated to Bergman. Courtesy of the Department of Archives, the National Library of Israel.

Moshe finds a connection between self-defense and autosuggestion.

In his Jiu-Jitsu book, Moshe advises a person who freezes in fear to use autosuggestion to free his body to move, and in a footnote offers details of the book, *Autosuggestion.*

In a later version of his Jiu-Jitsu book he published in French, *La Défense du Faible Contre L'Agreassur* (Edition Chiron, 1935), he directed the reader to *L'autosuggestion* by Charles Baudoin and *Le Maîtrise de Soi-même* by Émile Coué.

We are interested in the connection Moshe makes between the conscious and the unconscious, which is found in his explanation that the contents of the unconscious are accumulated by study, learning, and diligence. In other words, there is continuing feedback throughout life between the conscious and the unconscious. Moshe maintained that using natural unconscious reactions forms good foundation for conscious learning.

In his draft for the English version of his Jiu-Jitsu book (never published), Moshe wrote:

> The first movement of each encounter is the most natural movement dictated by the instinct of conservation or self-defense. It will always be the movement which is called forth in spite of oneself, almost as a reflex.
>
> Experience shows that a comparatively short period of training is amply sufficient to learn how to continue the counter which was already begun, and how to carry it out effectively.
>
> The contact between the part of the body which produces the first instinctive movement and the limb of the aggressor or his weapon calls forth the impulsion that urges you to continue.

Moshe's brilliant ideas are described clearly in the interview with Dennis Leri in San Francisco in 1977. Here is part of it:

And then I went and took a group of people and I took a knife and I attacked each of them ... And I retained their first move ... he substitutes an arm for the head, the throat, the back ... So that was the idea, to find out what was the first movement one does. And I built a system of defense for any sort of attack where the first movement is not what you think to do, what you decide to do, but what you actually do when you are frightened ... we will train the people so that end of the first spontaneous movement is where we must start ... We'll train them three months like we did before, give them a year off without training regularly, and then a year afterwards, try to attack again. And of course, the year afterwards, the first defensive movement they did, once they did their spontaneous first movement, was the continuation of that first movement. It was a remarkable thing.

Moshe demonstrating an instinctive movement.
Photo from the self-defense book.

Moshe relied on the valid treasure of the unconscious and even if a person does not practice regularly, the spontaneous action awakens the body to complete the defense movement. As stated, Moshe understood the importance of nourishing, through learning and diligence, from the conscious to the unconscious. He wrote about the subject in his book from 1942, *Practical Unarmed Combat*:

> The ultimate value of an exercise lies in the action your body will perform spontaneously, without conscious effort, long after you have forgotten how, when, and where you have learned it. The operation you have exercised repeatedly, rather than what you had in mind, is voluntarily executed by the physical body and is readily reproduced in spite of yourself.

Moshe's idea of using natural reactions as the basis for learning was used by the Haganna organization. The group, which developed Kapap, a face-to-face combat method, in 1942, adopted it as a basic principle. The Haganna used Kapap until the establishment of the state of Israel in 1948.

It is difficult for me to lay down my pen. I would like to go on writing, but in summary, as a researcher into the roots of the *Feldenkrais Method*, I would like to say that I am often astounded by new discoveries of situations and events that occurred in Moshe's life and how he transformed them into opportunities that delineated the trajectory on which he advanced towards developing his life's work.

It seems the connecting strands of Moshe's life offer us a semblance of an answer to the recurring question of when and how Moshe developed the method that bears his name.

—Moti Nativ, *Feldenkrais* Practitioner, Shihan in the Bujinkan School of Budo Taijutsu, Tel Aviv, Israel

Foreword

Émile Coué, the creator of the *Nancy Second School of Thought*[3] and the founder and manager of the Institute of Mental Health, died on July 2, 1926, in Nancy, France. Coué was one of the quintessential humanistic benefactors of our times. His father was a minor railroad civil servant. In 1857, under his father's influence, he became a pharmacist in his hometown of Troyes.

At the age of twenty-eight, Coué first came to know the physicians, students of the "First School of Nancy," who daringly cured people using hypnosis. Coué learned from them and practiced this method, which subsequently became immensely popular.

In 1885 he cured a girl who was unable to digest her food and from time to time would vomit it. Coué knew her mother since she had been coming to his pharmacy for many months to pick up an assortment of medications for her daughter. He suggested curing her daughter using hypnosis. The mother assented and Coué managed to cure the girl immediately.

Coué practiced hypnosis for sixteen years until he realized that it was possible to substitute suggestion, which worked just as well, without putting the patient to sleep, as done in hypnosis. However, he developed his "Coué Method" only after realizing that suggestion is effective only if it is self-suggestion and that it is not the doctor who heals the patient by hypnosis, but rather the patient who heals himself by autosuggestion. The overriding principle to the understanding of hypnosis is, according to Coué: "There is no suggestion without autosuggestion."

Suggestion and hypnosis are not processes of *transferring* a thought or a will from one person to another. Autosuggestion awakens within us an internal process whereby we influence ourselves.

An example of this can be seen as follows: there are occasions when the person does not fully understand what the hypnotist means and instead of doing what the hypnotist intended, he does what he *thinks* the hypnotists means. Therefore, the action taken comes not from the hypnotist's directive, but from the patient's own autosuggestion.

The person being hypnotized is passive only during the act of receptivity while being awakened from the trance state, but the final concrete act of awakening is his own.

Autosuggestion manifests itself regularly in our daily lives. Take a plank ten meters long by twenty-five centimeters wide and place it on the floor, then walk along its full length.

No one will falter while doing this. However, if the same plank is suspended in the air between two towers, no one will dare to walk on it because everyone believes they will fall, and they will indeed fall. Every idea strives to be fulfilled and provides the motivating force for its fulfillment. Coué proved the truth of his idea by simple experiments:

If I hold a plumb line suspended above a sheet of paper spread on the table that has a circle drawn on it with two diameters in the shape of a cross, marked AB and CD, the plumb line will sway in the direction of my thinking—be it in the AB or the CD direction. My thought will therefore act to direct the sway of the plumb line. This will occur even if I strain to maintain the vertical. My thought and imagination are stronger than my willpower.

This, then, is Coué's great principle: Imagination has higher priority and preference over willpower.

Any exercise of willpower results in failure if unaccompanied by imagination and faith. Coué liked to use the example of a man learning to ride a bicycle who, upon seeing a rock in his path, tries to avoid it by veering to the side. His effort only brings about the very result he was attempting to forestall and he ends up riding directly toward the rock.

Charles Baudouin[4] defined this psychological law as "the law of reversed effort." Any straining of the will that is in opposition to the imagined process will cause damage. This idea is in accord with Henri-Louis Bergson's[5] philosophy, which states that willpower and intelligence are merely superficial expressions of the mind whereas their deeper manifestations are imagination and instinct. As surface has no effect on depth, similarly, willpower will not alter the process of imagination. Therefore, our conscious will does not bring about actionable suggestions. Educating the imagination is more important than educating the will. Man fulfills in his life what his imagination directs him to do.

Each of us contains his life's image within himself. The course of our lives expresses and fulfills this image. Based upon this premise, Coué encouraged people to nurture their highest mental and spiritual faculties.

Many educators mock the faculties of imagination and think that imagination is just a function of an immature mind—a kind of childish, transitional stage. Coué came to understand the value of these twilight-like conditions. Here is where the importance of skill comes to the fore and brings us to the state in which our hidden mental powers rise from below.

Coué averred that if we wish to nurture our conscious lives, we should not ridicule those moments when we daydream, in which we remove from ourselves the strains and tensions of our souls, thus releasing the deep wellspring of our powerful potential, allowing it to rise to the surface.

These transitional states of consciousness are most effective in educating our faculties and autosuggestion can influence us during such intermediate states of waking and sleeping. What cannot be accomplished by conscious willpower and exertion will be accomplished by autosuggestion. This, then, is the notion upon which Coué based his therapeutic method.

He surmised that the origins of many illnesses that enslave us are based solely in imagination. The actions generated by these images can be changed by replacing the negative images with positive ones whose function is to support and assist. Coué, therefore, advised his patients to say to themselves: "Day by day, in every way, I am getting better and better."

These "prayer like" words are to be repeated twenty times at night just before falling asleep when one is drowsy, and in the morning upon awakening, when one is still half asleep. The repetitive monotony of the words will act on the mind below the level of conscious awareness to heal and raise the level of self confidence. In addition, the person who is emotionally depressed is to repeat to himself many times, "This will pass, this will pass," without interruption (in order to fend off any thoughts of despair). The formula he is to use must at all times be a positive one, without any negative connotations. He is not to say to himself: "I will not be weak," but instead will say, "I will be strong," and similar words, so as to prevent any intrusion of negative thoughts.

As a man tires during hiking, he will refresh himself by using the rhythm of his walking to induce a state of semi-sleep during which the suggestion of strength, persistence, and of being refreshed, will restore his energies. He is not to say, "I am not tired," but will say, "I am refreshed," and similar words.

Man's ability to induce upon himself the state of autosuggestion is an important factor that he can use to develop his strengths. Using suggestion one can improve memory.

One of Coué's students, Abramovsky (first name unknown), formulated an axiom whereby a person's energy level is related to his ability to bring himself to a state of autosuggestion.

Our lives are inundated with suggestions, emanating from a variety of sources: the government, the political party, newspapers, fashion, and society. They are all tools of suggestion, considered by many as being dangerous. Coué disagreed with this idea. Every suggestion is based upon autosuggestion. The weakness is not in the development of autosuggestion, but in the uncritical acceptance of suggestions from others.

He differentiates between autosuggestion and suggestion imposed by others and therefore advocates teaching school children to use the powers of autosuggestion. The educator must impress upon his students one suggestion: not to accept ideas from others before examining them. These days when most educators are not aware of the powers of suggestion, the children's world is filled with incorrect suggestions. The teacher tells the child: "You are lazy!" This is the type of suggestion that brings about the opposite of the intended effect. In contrast, Professor Baudouin points to the excellence of a teacher who, at the beginning of the week, wrote on the blackboard: "These are the things we are deciding for the coming week..." and in this manner impressed upon the children positive, strong, and useful suggestions. (The student should not say to himself, "I want to be diligent," but should say, "I will be diligent," etc.)

Suggestion has a very powerful effect on everything concerned with emotion. William James[6] said: "We don't cry because we are sad, we are sad because we cry." In other words, the movements of the body have an active, suggestive effect on the spirit. Body and mind affect each other, just as parts of an electric induction machine enhance the actions of each other. Goethe advised people to laugh even without a specific reason because the laughter in and of itself brings about the state of joy. Bodily movements act suggestively just like emotional images.

We cannot imagine an emotional state without in some way being in that state. An actor on the stage who is expressing an emotional state will impose upon himself a suggestive transformation into the person he is to portray. His artistic talent is dependent upon his ability to induce himself into the required act of autosuggestion.

These things are known. Coué, who taught people to use auto-suggestion, would tell his patients, who came to Nancy by the thousands to be cured by him (even of illnesses of organic origin), "I have no magnetic powers. I am not a miracle worker. I only want to teach you to heal yourselves."

Many preceded him in this field of knowledge. Suggestion and autosuggestion are present in all primitive societies in their traditions of magic ceremonies, and in "enlightened" civilizations in their superstitious beliefs. From the educational and psychological aspect, Coué's method excels in that it gives greater value to the power of the imagination than to the power of conscious will.

"The law of reversed effort" is undoubtedly a law of great educational and psychological value.

—Professor Hugo Bergman, Jerusalem, April 20, 1930

Preface

We have today about one hundred varieties of therapeutic methods dealing with disturbances and psychosomatic mental illnesses. Several of them are very sophisticated and have been adopted with enthusiasm by major medical schools and internationally known hospitals. Given this, the reader may very well be surprised and ask: What is the purpose in reviving an additional method, that of Emile Coué, in which the principal technique is simply instructing the patient to sense that he feels better?

Is there any reason to expect that this method of autosuggestion (that was at one time so popular, but is today almost completely forgotten), will be more successful than modern, tested, and validated techniques? Is autosuggestion based on a reasonable theoretical model and does it rest on an array of supporting evidence? And if autosuggestion does have meaning and value as a therapeutic method, why is it that Coué and the hypotheses on which his method is based have not earned any substantive scientific recognition? How are we to understand that even Coué's huge popularity did not grant him a semblance, albeit limited, of scientific recognition?

Our answers to these questions are very simple.

It is not good for a scientist to be a prophet, i.e., to be able, through the experience of his work, to foresee a reality that science has not yet deemed to be sufficiently valid. The scientific establishment tends to ignore discoveries that do not fit the accepted theories of their time and which are not amenable to validation by current accepted methods and techniques such as the scientific games of proof and disproof. The situation for the prophet-scientist is worse if his discovery, unaccepted by his peers, gains wide popularity and acceptance by the general public. In such instances the discovery is treated as insignificant and valueless and the discoverer usually earns the title of charlatan.

At various times in their lives acclaimed researchers such as Galileo and Freud were obliged to endure the stain of being labeled charlatans. However, a few of them, being so ahead of their times, departed from this world without achieving even a modicum of scientific recognition. Coué was one of those few. While Coué's treatment helped many thousands of people in the Western world, the medical establishment of that period, with the exception of one or two supporters, viewed his method, in the best of circumstances, as a silly trend, and in the worst as fraud. In fact, they could not have reached a different conclusion because his basic idea did not fit two of the fundamental scientific tenets of disease of that time, which not only provided the theoretical basis of disease, but were also able to buttress those theories based upon the numerous clinical successes substantiating those theories.

These two tenets were the physiological theory of disease and the psychoanalytical or depth psychology approaches. In other words, it was necessary to reject Coué's presumption that thought can be a therapeutic factor because he was unable to explain in a convincing way how the image of feeling good could effect physiological processes such as reducing pain or the ability to contend with the challenges of complexes in the Freudian sense. Moreover, Coué was unable to point to any peer-reviewed replicated research demonstrating that the contents of a particular thought have a very specific effect on the body of the thinker.

It is clear that were it not for reasonable hypotheses and experimental proofs, which are the prerequisites for scientific acceptance, science would collapse under the weight of false ideas, invalid opinions, or weird notions having no logical basis, as Coué's ideas were perceived to be.

In light of the absence of scientific underpinning, and although Coué was justifiably widely known as the most successful healer at the beginning of the twentieth century, this popularity did not help in bringing his life's work into the canons of known medical knowledge. After his death in 1926, his students and patients continued to apply the method they had learned from their teacher, but the principles at the basis of his method sank into oblivion

Today, fifty years after the death of Coué, circumstances have completely changed. Psychological and physiological research, unrelated to Coué's work, has provided convincing scientific proof supporting Coué's fundamental ideas.

Reviving the memory of Coué's work is not just a matter of historical justice, but contains benefits for medical and behavioral sciences and for the wellbeing of all people. Even today, Coué's work contributes much to currently accepted therapeutic approaches. In other words, the prophet of fifty years ago is still a scientific pioneer today.

Illustrating experimental evidence supporting Coué's suppositions would require much more space than is reasonably warranted in a preface, but a few examples will suffice to serve as witness that Coué's intuitive ideas have a solid scientific basis.

Let us take the assumption that thinking has the power not only to exercise an effect on mood, but can also cause physiological changes. As mentioned above, this notion was thought to be without merit and the self-deceptive product of a mind devoid of critical thinking. The position taken was that physiological changes are fundamentally autonomic. While autonomic changes have the power to create and to influence cognitive activity, thinking, in and of itself, and thought in particular, cannot in any way determine the electrochemical chain of processes that constitute life.

And then, several years ago, experimental proof demonstrated that if a person expects an event to take place, that expectation creates significant changes in the pattern of his brain waves. Moreover, if that expectation ceases, the electrical wave map changes, too. Given that an imagined event is present only in the field of imagined thought, it follows that the thought process itself caused the change in the wave pattern. Obviously, there are still conservative neurophysiologists who hold the view that the expectations themselves are strictly physiological changes brought about by other physiological processes, which are not effected by any cognitive conclusive processes. But this assumption, popular as it may be, is not in itself a purely scientific point of view because there is not a shred of evidence indicating that cognitive and logical inferences are caused by certain physiological response patterns. There are, however, numerous proofs supporting the influence of awareness on life processes.

In this regard, it is unimportant whether the knowledge is derived from the environment or from logical inference, or concluded as a result of deductive reasoning. What is important is to see that science, by recognizing psychosomatic influences on informational content, has provided the basis and justification for Coué's most fundamental argument.

A different idea of Coué's, one that has great importance beyond the parameters of autosuggestion, has to do with using humility as a technical tool in rendering advice. Coué advised his patients not to focus on sudden or gradual release from their illnesses or pains, but to imagine only the positive results of getting better and better. The argument that the positive can have much greater impact on change than the negative did not fit the educational model nor that of adapting to and accepting one's life circumstances, which was current in European circles of the time.

In accordance with homeostatic principles, the organism starts to act, or changes the way it acts, in order to lower discomfort caused by a bias, imbalance, or inability to adapt. It followed, therefore, that it was necessary to avoid the negative and the suffering and to punish the motivating source generating the negative states.

Freud recognized the huge attraction of comfort and pleasure, but described the pleasure principle as unrealistic and as a factor inevitably producing disease and, as such, categorized it as belonging to the primitive subconscious aspect of personality. In summary, psychoanalytical therapy aimed at bringing the patient to behave in accordance with reality and not in accordance with the pleasure principle. Consequently, psychoanalysis was not able to stress the advantages of striving for pleasure, despite the fact that in theory, psychoanalysis could have stressed this aspect and indeed, it has been criticized by its opponents precisely for this lack.

Edward Thorndike, the American scholar who experimented to find out how animals learn, noticed that rewards have a much greater effect on the learning ability of animals than punishment, the effect of which is almost negligible.

But his experiments, which were probably unknown to Coué, were at that time not yet replicated by other scientists and, moreover, lacked a reasonable theoretical framework. It was only later, at about the time of Coué's death, that solid proof became available, namely that the expectation of reward promotes learning and other permanent character changes more than does the fear of suffering and punishment. These proofs were, however, not convincing enough for parents, educators, and judges.

It is worth noting that the ideas behind Coué's teachings, to focus on the positive, are of significantly broader psychological application when compared to the behaviorist idea of rewards. A person suffering severe pain imagines the potential for reducing or eliminating the pain as being the greatest possible reward. And, indeed, reduction of pain is a positive benefit and is the reason the patient is drawn towards imagining the pain abating.

But, by so doing, he remains engaged with the pain! Coué's instruction not to imagine, "My pain is lessening," but, for example, to imagine, "I am feeling better," or "My condition is getting better and better from minute to minute," creates a sharp veering away from the pain and suffering that is controlling the person. In fact, the instruction demands ignoring something that is present, real, and intensely felt.

From a psychological standpoint, can such a change of direction be possible? In Coué's lifetime the predominant viewpoint was that perception was more or less automatic. It was believed that people's perceptual ability falls more or less within the boundaries of their sensory organs—at least regarding events of the most intense, physically and physiologically.

Only recently have scientists successfully demonstrated that perceptual expansion improves in relation to the *attentional* level and is regulated in accordance with ideas and assumptions about the percept.

Furthermore, experiments have proven that when a person is distracted by an instruction to attend to something else, he will not notice something that is clearly there, right in front of his eyes.

Accordingly, it would be correct to say that Coué's fundamental assertion not only utilizes the effect of the positive, but exploits the power of attentiveness. In other words, that special human talent enabling a person to select, within certain fairly broad parameters, those realities within which he wishes to be.

The fact that proof of superior effectiveness of reward over punishment is more effective, and that thought content can affect physiological processes, is not sufficient to support the conclusion that imagined rewards give rise to feelings similar to those of receiving actual material rewards, or that thinking of better life conditions or improved health does in fact improve health.

Numerous proofs exist in the psychological field demonstrating that imagination does have the power to stimulate emotions. One well known example is the "placebo" effect. Patients who receive a placebo, i.e., a medication that contains only an ineffective ingredient such as a smidgen of salt but is presented to them as a relaxant, relax physiologically as well as psychologically, exactly like the group that received a medication actually containing the listed medicinal components.

The difference between the placebo and the actual medication is that the effect of the placebo wears off faster than the effect of the medication.

Another example is that people watching a catastrophic accident on TV who believe the accident did, in fact, happen, respond emotionally at similar physiological and psychological levels as people who watch the same film but believe that it was just a film aired by the network.

Experiments such as these offer scientific support for what is known empirically by any person who experiences actual hunger pangs while imagining a tasty meal, or becomes sexually aroused when imagining sexual activity whether in the waking state or in a dream. It follows then that Coué was correct in assuming that positive imaginings of being healthier lead to more pleasant feelings similar to actually being healthy.

Moreover, such imagining would actually reduce the discomfort just as the placebo pill that is offered for headache reduces or eliminates that pain.

But is it possible to rely on Coué's clinical observations with regard to real diseases that are mostly psychosomatic? Is there a basis for the idea that autosuggestion *per se* has healing effects such as Coué and his students have claimed? Clinical observations are, by their nature, less reliable than verifiable trials, but the cumulative clinical evidence of many years, while being indirect, is quite convincing. Coué presumed that the process leading to positive therapeutic outcome is hypnosis, applied in the form of auto-hypnosis. He maintained that all hypnosis is auto-hypnosis.

Serious observational evidence indicating the various effects of hypnosis was present in abundance even before Coué's time. From much accumulated experience, Coué was able to learn that hypnosis can have an effect on thought, memory, motor activity, pain sensation, hemorrhaging, and most, if not all, the autonomic functions of the body. There was, however, no convincing evidence supporting the hypothesis that auto- or self-suggestions can produce similar effects.

Recognition that some action on the part of the hypnotee was required for hypnosis to take effect came about because even the most accomplished hypnotist is unable to hypnotize a person against his will.

During the last fifty years scientists conducting experiments in hypnosis have not succeeded in developing a widely accepted explanation for the hypnotic effect. They have not even arrived at a consensus determining the most effective technique for inducing hypnosis.

But the excellent work of T. K. Barber[8] and his students clarifies without a shadow of doubt that it is possible to create all, or most, hypnotic manifestations without the participation of the hypnotist in the classic sense of the word, and without utilizing any of the multiple hypnotic techniques. They showed that it was enough to rely on cognitive means, i.e., to persuade the person to use his imaging abilities in order to achieve the result that was dependent on the hypnotic state. Moreover, obstetricians who use hypnosis in alleviating or eliminating the pain of childbirth have found that a woman who has learned how to enter into a hypnotic state can easily give herself the requisite signals to induce self-hypnosis.

Finally, it is worth noting that research studies of the last few years on the physiological effects of relaxation have found significant changes in heart rate and blood pressure, especially in situations of relaxation under the control of the person himself, such as during transcendental meditation. Such marked physiological changes are difficult to attain even with classic hypnosis.

And from this it is evident that what is most needed is the belief that the method being utilized is the most efficient one, regardless of whether it is hypnosis, autosuggestion, meditation, or autogenic training.

Certainly, all of this does not prove that the processes involved in hypnosis versus self-hypnosis are identical, especially since neither of them is, as yet, fully understood. However, in practical terms, the observations and studies cited above show that from a therapeutic point of view, hypnosis and autosuggestion are of equal value, exactly as Coué justifiably claimed them to be.

But it seems that Coué would not have been able to treat so many people successfully without having inserted specific and important additions to the induction practices of hypnosis or autosuggestion, an addition that is in our opinion unique and revolutionary. Instead of telling his patients exactly what to think about and what to imagine, he gave them instructions with the widest possible boundaries, giving the patient free rein to furnish the particulars, the personal details based upon tenets of "feeling better" or "feeling good."

Coué clearly emphasized that specific autosuggestions related to deficiencies or specific illnesses are less effective than the general formula that has become a kind of aphorism: "From day to day, I am becoming better and better, in every way."

By emphasizing a general formulation, Coué on the one hand set himself against the psychological establishment of his time that insisted on precise, detailed instructions. On the other hand, he avoided being ensnared in the mistaken, rooted practices of standardized diagnosis and treatment designed to change behaviors on a psychological basis. This is a very serious mistake because the same circumstances seen by one person as vital to his wellbeing may, for another person, be the source of his ill-being. It is no exaggeration that the concepts of "feeling good" or "be healthy" have as many meanings as the number of people using them.

In Coué's day, meanings had only philosophical interpretations, theories that did not offer differentiations or impart an ability to compare them one with another. Hence it was not possible to define reasonably and conclusively a concept of health or of wellbeing that would apply to all or most patients.

Instead of treading the same old path taken by the psychologists and psychiatrists of his time who opted to apply the same standard coinage, Coué preferred to have his patients determine for themselves what constitutes good health, wellbeing, or improvement of their life circumstances. Of course, if the patient's perception of health was so neurotically distorted as to be hazardous, he would refer the patient to a psychiatrist.

Advances that have taken place in our times with regard to measurement and change of meaning[9] would have enabled Coué to guide his patients to discover concepts of health that would have been congruent with their beliefs and values with regard to themselves and their lives, as well as with their physiological needs. Even so, the actual discovery would have been left as a personal aim of the patient to be performed every week or even daily, in accordance with his own preferences and objective constraints.

And so we are faced with Coué's great contribution, perhaps his greatest: he tried to prevent the trend leading toward ever increasing dependency on psychological and medical help. With his patients he attempted to thwart the development of dependency. Directly and indirectly, he reminded his patients that they would have to pay for the consequences of their diseases because the responsibility of caring for their health is their own.

Physicians looking to play God, who are too arrogant or lazy to have their patients become partners in their own care will tend, even these days, to reject this approach to maintaining health and wellbeing. But this is to be understood: it is possible to effectively challenge the growing perils to health emanating from chemical pollution and the social and psychological strife typical of our times only if every person becomes knowledgeable and aware of the fact that he can, on his own, do much for his own health bodily, mentally, and socially.

Reducing dependency by actively sharing responsibility always acts to reduce anxiety as well. If we examine and interpret the system of thought, imagination, and autosuggestion in this light, Coué's method appears to be extremely valuable, much more than Coué would or could have surmised in his lifetime.

—Professors Hans Kreitler and Shulamit Kreitler[7]
Tel Aviv, Israel, February, 1977

Thinking and Doing

Dedicated to the immigrants by the translator, Dr. M. Feldenkrais, Tel Aviv, 1929

The Unconscious as Executor

In the previous chapters we dealt with the unconscious and with autosuggestion insofar as they impacted on abnormal life: we saw their effect on disease, anxiety, crime, and generally on all distortions of normative behavior.

On the other hand, we have barely touched upon the ways we can perfect the healthy by means of elevating man's inherent capabilities and improving them. We have occupied ourselves with the means needed by man to avoid living lives of misery. We tried to lighten the heavy burden weighing down the sick in any kind of illnesses.

In this chapter, we will explore this issue and see if we can take it a step forward. Using examples from real life, we will demonstrate that using autosuggestion we can achieve far superior results rather than merely being in a condition no worse than someone else's.

We have already shown that in human beings the unconscious is far more in control of all aspects involving vital bodily processes. The unconscious knows all: what comes first and what comes later. It organizes digestion, assimilation, respiration and the like. In short, the unconscious is the final arbiter, the primary authority. However, when we touch upon the external aspects of human life, such as the struggle with nature and the need to control the environment, it becomes necessary to clarify this matter further. It is imperative to demonstrate that the unconscious mind has a significant role to play in the actions of the conscious mind.

Let us take a simple, familiar example: a person living on the upper floor of a walkup building ascends and descends the stairs many times daily. He never stumbles or misses a step even at night when the staircase is dark. He climbs the steps rapidly without stumbling or groping to find the next step down or up. If we ask him how many steps he climbs, we will not be surprised to hear that he does not know. This is common and we have all had similar experiences. If asked how we climb and descend these steps without knowing how many there are, we answer, "This is a simple matter, I just do it," but such an answer does not explain it.

The unconscious records every movement we make, every thought that passes through our minds. As we repeatedly climb the steps from one landing to the next, our unconscious mind notes the number of leg movements we perform during each ascent or descent. We are not aware of this mental recording process, nor are we aware of how our unconscious utilizes its experience as it counts, albeit not by the use of numerical symbols. The proof lies in the fact that there are times when, even though we have not made any mental effort to count the steps, we can access this number and bring it to our conscious awareness. The unavoidable conclusion is that the unconscious learns from experience.

If physically attacked, few people can explain why they made this or that movement to protect themselves. Most people do not know specifically where their solar plexus is located, and yet the moment a person fears he is about to be attacked, he will bend forward slightly, without conscious awareness, and by so doing will protect his vulnerable solar plexus with his ribs.

When faced with the prospect of being beaten over the head with a stick, it is doubtful if many people know that the bony forehead is stronger than the bones of the back of the head—or that a blow around the ears is more dangerous than to other parts of the skull, yet every person covers his head in a way that protects those vulnerable parts and permits the forehead to suffer the brunt of the blow.

Not everyone would react consciously in the above manner. Not everyone would know how to do it, or be capable of deciding to do it. Moreover our unconscious mind is the repository not only of our own personal memories and experiences, but also of those of our fathers and forefathers over many generations of experience and repetition. The most effective protective movement pattern became determined and fixed so that it takes place despite our conscious will.

Without paying close attention, we will not be able to understand or discern the fine adaptations the unconscious mind produces in the defensive actions taken by that part of the body. For example, a child running away to escape a bully will arch his back and push his chest forward so as to distance his back from the blow he feels is being aimed at him. But the moment his tormentor reaches him, he will round his back like a cat. In so doing he creates a bow that is more rigid than a straight line, thereby protecting his heart and lungs.

At that moment, the child is obviously far from understanding the purpose of his movements, moreover he does not understand the function of the rest of his body, either, because these movements are determined by his unconscious mind, sometimes based on his own personal experience, and sometimes on the basis of the accumulated experience of generations past.

The opposite movement will occur if a person feels the prick of a knife in his back. He will arch his back creating an impenetrable bony barrier, the ribs bunching close to one another. Moreover, by so doing, he will distance that part of himself from the threatening knife. The attacker, unable to extricate his weapon, may even leave his knife in the victim's body wedged tightly between the ribs. This explains the apparent miracle in which many victims, who have been stabbed numerous times, survive, despite not being very strong individuals. We see then that the unconscious mind is a veritable storehouse of memories and knowledge that can become available to us only through diligent observation, study, experience, and much effort.

But the role of the unconscious is not limited to memorizing, storing, and then making its knowledge available upon demand; its creative ability is vast. It uses its treasured experience to reform, to reconfigure and create new varieties that are beyond the ability of most people using their mental faculties on a conscious level.

Let us take the long jump as an example. When running in order to jump, some people push off from the ground with their left leg and swing the right leg forward in the air while others do the opposite. In preparation for the jump, the person starts running from a distance in order to gain sufficient momentum, enabling him to jump farther, and when he starts running he needs to know with which leg to initiate the run so as to arrive at the take-off point with the leg he is in the habit of using for that action.

We will not be mistaken if we say that ninety-nine out of a hundred jumpers do not know that they must take an even number of strides during the run in order to arrive at the take-off point with the same push-off leg they used when they started the run, and an odd number of strides to arrive at the take-off point with the swing leg. In addition, if we consider that the jumper needs to estimate the number of steps he must take to the take-off spot and only then to decide with which leg to initiate the jump, we will have to acknowledge that we did not exaggerate in saying that few people can calculate all this on a conscious level. If we try to calculate this on a conscious level we find it a difficult undertaking, one in which we would most often be wrong, whereas the unconscious performs this task almost flawlessly. There is no need to prove that these calculations are being done, the results are proof enough.

Occasionally, the jumper realizes in mid-run that he will not reach the take-off point with the leg he normally uses for jumping. We see such runners correct their error while running, and "change feet" by taking a small skipping step, or by adding strides to change the sequence. Clearly something other than our conscious self is doing the calculating and correcting the error, if there is one, and who or what would that be, other than the unconscious?

It is worth mentioning that we know how to do many things in the most effective way when we rely on the unconscious. When we interfere with its working and permit the conscious mind to take over, we veer from one mistake to another. Moreover, we fail to understand the reason for the failure.

Here is an example: place a bottle on the table so that the top rim of the bottle will be either thirty centimeters lower or higher than the eye-level of the person doing this experiment. Place a box of matches or a cork on the bottle rim. The person will now step back about five steps and then raise his hand forward, aim at the cork, and run forward to topple the cork off the bottle. We will be surprised to see that no amount of precision in aiming the finger will avail, and even after several attempts, the cork will remain perched atop the bottle. However, if we give up the notion of aiming in advance and allow our arm to be free, we will find that we can run toward the bottle and knock off the cork any time we wish.

This seems to present us with a paradox: when we plan and aim, logically we should be able to dislodge the cork easily. At the very least we should be closer to our target than when we have freed our arm from the prepared position of aiming, but experience shows us that our success rate is significantly greater when we do not aim our hand in advance. Common sense tells us that the better we aim, the better we score, so why is this not so in our experiment?

If the task of delivering mail were assigned to the general manager of a post office instead of to the regular mailman, would he be able to perform it well? The manager does not know how to carry out the work of his staff, so when he tries to take their place he will only make a fool of himself. A wise manager will employ capable and loyal workers and after informing them what needs to be done, will move away and allow them to perform their duties without interference. If we examine this matter closely, we will discover the reason why we were unable to dislodge the cork from the top of the bottle when we did it by aiming our hand in advance.

We have determined that the concrete issue of aiming and hitting the target is a conscious act. Given that the eye and the target are two points connected in space on the same dimension, we can imagine the trajectory. When we add a third element, say a finger, a pistol, a rifle, or a bullet onto this trajectory, and have the third element move along this line in the direction of the target, we would expect to hit it, but that is not the case.

If the person who is aiming at a bird in a tree starts moving in the direction of the target, upon reaching the tree the barrel of the gun will be at the level of his eye. As he approaches the tree he does not change the position of his arm in relation to the ground and will not hit the top of the tree or the bird, just as we could not touch an object on the ground as we approach it, even though we are pointing at it, unless we bend down to pick it up.

Let us now examine what exactly happened in our experiment with the cork:

The constraint was that that the cork would be positioned approximately thirty centimeters below or above eye level as we stand at a distance of, say, four to five steps away from the bottle.

When we point our finger at the cork, our hand will be higher than the cork even though the bottle is beneath our eye level, and vice versa, our finger will be lower than the cork if the bottle is situated above our eye level. Obviously, when we think of aiming our finger, we are trying to maintain the position of our arm, hence the more we try to maintain our original aim and its position, the less likely we are to hit the target. But if our intention is to dislodge the cork and we refrain from consciously keeping our arm in any particular position, the unconscious mind takes over and makes whatever adjustments are necessary for the finger to reach the cork precisely and knock it off its perch.

Now we see that the unconscious knows how to execute what the conscious mind entrusts to it better than the conscious mind itself, which often does the exact opposite of what is required, without our even being aware of it. In particular, it is in circumstances in which the unconscious mind functions unhindered that we see that it is more effective and hence is to be preferred when carrying out executive actions.

Last in Deed, First in Thought[10]

What does "correct thinking" mean? In previous chapters we said that an idea that presented itself to our conscious mind, was accepted by it, and became a vital and consistent element in our life, is in and of itself spontaneous autosuggestion. If the accepted idea *a priori* was intended for the unconscious, it would be a case of persuasive or inductive autosuggestion. Accordingly, all the examples presented in the previous chapter were in and of themselves autosuggestions.

Self-autosuggestions are the most powerful and are executed at maximum speed, namely at the speed of thought. These suggestions are material for analysis, from which we may arrive at conclusions regarding all the other ideas we want to actualize. In autosuggestion we may examine several characteristics:

a. They are always thoughts, the contents of which are actions that have been completed. Thus, the long jumper will think of jumping in the safest way, seeing himself as a whole, etc. (One person will think of leaping from the take-off point, another may think how his body moves in the air...)

b. The thought is always singular. The thought or image being at that moment actualized is the only one being accepted or rejected by the unconscious. (This does not mean that during a relatively long period the person concerned with his safety has only one thought in his mind. He thinks very quickly, and the thoughts in his head follow each other but only serially, one after the other.) The one thought being implemented is the only one at that moment being accepted or rejected by the unconscious mind.

c. In all of these the element of will is absent as it relates to an urge or craving.[11] These three elements constitute the essence of autosuggestion. All autosuggestions that influence behavior are built upon these foundations. Any thought developed in accordance with this plan will be manifest in the unconscious and become realized in actual life. However, there are times when the "sentinel," as described by Freud, will prevent the passage of such a thought. Experience shows us that those thoughts that are accompanied by a yearning for the situation in which that craving is expressed are precisely the ones that the unconscious rejects.

"The sentinel" tells you: "Such and such can only be done by a person endowed with God's grace, but you have not yet reached that level." If we examine our thoughts honestly, we will discover that all those unfulfilled life aspirations contain within them such a thorn. The average person wanting to carry out an elegant motion will think at that very moment that such a movement can only be carried out by a naturally talented actor or dancer onstage and that he himself is surely not capable of doing it so well. And indeed, upon attempting it, it does not appear well done and he hears comments around him: "Aha! We have a new dancer here," or, "Take a look at this dandy," etc.

His movements did not turn out well because his thinking was not free of the impediment of urge. In our above example, the part of the movement unhampered by unrelated intrusive thoughts was performed, but the second part of the thinking—the beauty and grace of the motion—was lacking.

But are there not people in this world who move with elegance? Yes, there are, and these are people in whom the image of the movement arises in their brains without eliciting any conflicting thoughts that would weaken the power of the original thought.

A budding dancer is recognized in early childhood. She tries every single movement while other children at that young age who do not know how to think freely for themselves think that it is beneath them to imitate her. Other children may think of doing it only when they are older. With such excuses they opt out of exploring or experimenting (original thinking is not so prevalent at a very young age), i.e., the image of the movement does not manifest itself in their unconscious because it is accompanied by emotionally charged intrusive thoughts.

It follows then that even a person sound in mind and body may not know how to do a whole variety of things. The word "know" is not chosen lightly. If he knew how to think properly, he would undoubtedly succeed. We see many examples of this in daily life: a strong, healthy man watches a young man lifting a heavy weight. The young man looks small, perhaps feeble, yet he lifts the weight overhead and repeats it with ease. People who are watching turn their heads to look at the strong man but he, despite being much stronger than the young man, is unskilled in weight lifting and is unable to lift the weight above his waist.

He knows he is much stronger than the young man, so he excuses himself by telling the onlookers that at the moment his wrist is injured and painful, etc., but all these excuses will not help him raise the weight above his head. However, once he learns how to lift the weight he will do it very easily. It is not enough to be strong and have the potential ability. In order to implement a thought one has to know *how*.

We know how to do many things because they are common-place tasks and we have learned them from those who preceded us, but when we encounter something that is new to us on a personal level and is at times complex and difficult, we need to know how to direct our talents and utilize all of our abilities in order to attain our goal.

As a matter of fact, there is nothing new in what has been said so far and in what will follow, except that it has been assembled and crystallized into a coherent logical and useful whole. Most of the means we use were known and utilized by our forefathers.

For example, let us take the act of praying. As it is a common-place activity, we will refrain from investigating whether praying is a form of autosuggestion. Prayer always addresses the desired end without mentioning its opposite state, the existing situation. If the person is asking for a major request, he will preface it with a plea that his prayer be accepted. Even in this supplication it is easy to discern all the basic ideas we have emphasized earlier.

We have only to leaf through the *Tanakh*[12] to find ample support for what we have been saying. For example, we read in Chronicles 2, Chapter 6, verses 19-21:

[19] Have respect therefore to the prayer of thy servant, and to his supplication, O LORD my God, to hearken unto the cry and the prayer which thy servant prayeth before thee:

[20] That thine eyes may be open upon this house day and night, upon the place whereof thou hast said that thou wouldest put thy name there; to hearken unto the prayer which thy servant prayeth toward this place.

[21] Hearken therefore unto the supplications of thy servant, and of thy people Israel, which they shall make toward this place: hear thou from thy dwelling place, even from heaven; and when thou hearest, forgive.

Isn't this autosuggestion a preface for the more important request that is to follow, one that may not necessarily be fulfilled? And what would be the most appropriate time for autosuggestion? This too was known: "And this is the path thou shalt follow, and the deed thou shalt do to accustom thyself to guard against all sin; In the morning upon awakening thou shalt scrutinize thine actions and thou shalt not veer from the path even one step." (The basis for the answer of the *Chasid* [the righteous], our Rabbi Yonah[13]).

And another example: "And you shall scrutinize your actions morning and night. And in this will all of your days be in repentance." The missive of "The Ramban"[14] to his son.[15]

(Translator's note: The above is a portion from King Solomon's prayer dedicating the temple he built to God in Jerusalem. circa 840 BCE.)

If you say that the religious feeling of devotion in praying emerges of its own accord, even when not emanating from the heart—our elders differed, and exhorted us to pray with intention. They spoke of this repeatedly and instructed the nation in it:

Our Rabbi Sa'adia Gaon[16] wrote: "He who prays without heartfelt intention will not have his prayer heard." There are many such examples. Rabbi Eliezer[17] said: "Prayer is greater than good deeds" (Berakhot, 32b), meaning that prayer distills, purifies, and refines the soul. As such, prayer is more valuable than one good deed or another.

But suggestion is not the exclusive province of people who pray. Athletes, artists, actors, all use autosuggestion in the full meaning of the word without being aware of it and possibly because of that, they achieve superb results, since that is the way these suggestions resemble authentic autosuggestions.

The sportsman sees himself winning, he sees himself achieving his goal and these ideas become reality. Nurmi,[18] the long distance runner, is an interesting example. He knows exactly what will occur long before the race and announces it in public, i.e., he thinks of the win as a *fait accompli* and as this image passes before his eyes, it manifests itself in life.[19]

It is worthwhile noting that common opinion in this regard is totally in error. Most people think that running ten kilometers is hard work. They think this because they themselves strain in their running while Nurmi simply runs. They think that it is hard to run, but Nurmi thinks that this time he will run faster than ever before. It is reasonable to say that for this reason so few runners were able to catch up with him. All other explanations are trivial in relation to this main one. Training and exercise do help, but they are not the most important reasons.

Sir Robert Baden-Powell[20] tells of the famous tennis player Eustace Miles[21] who never exercises and does not prepare for the tournament but is always ready and able to defend his title. This, then, is the ideal situation that all athletes should strive for, yet this is where the most fundamental error is usually made.

With the best of intentions, physical educators and trainers impress upon their athletes the necessity of exercise without respite and impose upon them the idea that there can be no competition without rigorous training because if a person stops training prior to a race he is bound to lose. There is no doubt that systematic training assures improvement, but we must remember that exercise leaves an imprint that is not erased so quickly. A break in training for a few years will undoubtedly have a significant effect, but an intermission of a couple of months will not only not reduce or diminish anything, with the proper approach it will even improve performance. Constant repetition of the same mistake brings the athlete to a state where he no longer believes in his ability, loses his confidence, and in fact performs less well.

Every trainer has certainly encountered other athletes or trainers who pay too much attention to their breathing while they train. Such people often reach a condition in which cold sweat covers their faces and their hearts beat so hard that they are forced to stop soon after making light, regular movements performed in the context of exercising.

Such a person probably read somewhere or heard from a teacher about the importance of breathing properly while exercising. He may even have heard that exercising without breathing, or breathing improperly, is more harmful than helpful. At that moment he may even have thought, consciously, that since his lungs were not in the best of condition, he should take extra care when exercising. Since this idea gnawed at his mind, dragging after it similar associations, it was assimilated by the unconscious and manifested itself in reality. He experienced all the symptoms that are brought about by improper breathing.

So we see that those who think that exercise improves breathing will excel while those who think differently while doing exactly the same exercise routines strain their bodies and become bitterly disappointed. This is not a trivial matter. Freud, in his *General Introduction to Psychoanalysis,* said: "Incomplete clarity will often bring about traumatic results."[22] So we see that it is not the specific exercise *per se* that brings about the improvement. We have seen some people who, when doing exactly the same exercise not only did they not help themselves, but they may have harmed themselves simply by incorrect thinking. Just as we cannot say what sweetens the tea, the sugar or the stirring of it, similarly we cannot say what is preferred: the thought or the exercise. It is clear that both are needed. Just as the sugar and the stirring will sweeten the tea, correct thinking and doing will bring about the desired result easily and quickly.

The actor on stage uses autosuggestion, too. We can say that it is the acting that creates the autosuggestion. The very act of changing his appearance, of allowing known aspects of his character to be revealed while inhibiting others so that they remain hidden from critical observers, of adopting a different voice, using unfamiliar gestures, of thinking in unusual ways, these are not things one can do unless one is an actor, i.e., a person who knows how to actualize thoughts embedded in his unconscious mind instantly, without hesitating or doubting himself, without the resistance of obstructing associations. The actor trains himself in this, he wraps himself up in the very spirit of the person whose role he is playing. He does this behind the scenes, by reviewing and thinking about all that is to transpire on the stage. Or, he may think about the main scenes and the lines he is to say, prior to stepping onto the stage, i.e., he "enters the role." Close examination will demonstrate the great value of the unconscious and of autosuggestion in all of these matters.

Even before stepping onto the stage the actor reveals something of the unconscious, every actor in his own way. One will stride back and forth, another will sit, yet another will lie down, one will shut his eyes, another will fix his gaze on some distant point, each one in accordance with his inclination and experience. Now he dwells upon the subject matter he is to portray and envisions the salient characteristics of the person he is to play on stage, maybe also some lesser sections of the act. These thoughts will embed themselves in his unconscious and in this manner will attach themselves to the multitude of items stored in his memory.

This is an important place in which to clarify these interesting and ubiquitous things because most people do not bother to explain them. There are occasions when, in the middle of a scene that he has played many times, an actor will suddenly substitute a word that is different from the one he usually uses. It can change the content of his utterance because this new word, previously unconnected, now touches upon nuances in his unconscious, becomes organically related with his own personality and appears as if on its own. This happens in a similar way with respect to movement, a look, etc. In his biography, Feodor Chaliapin[23] tells an interesting story. Although "Ivan the Terrible" was the name of the character he was to portray, the element of terror was completely lacking. It was only after Savva Mamontov[24] helped him to understand this that the full meaning of the word came to life for him and he was able to sing the role that became one of the hallmarks of his repertoire.

A young, talented, but inexperienced performer mocks a critic who wrote a review extolling his performance as genuinely expressing the suffering of the nation, and who, in that word, or in that tone, voiced the anguished moans of the people. The inexperienced artist laughs, saying, "While acting I never thought about the pain, the suffering, or the anguished moan. The reviewer is philosophizing, and is seeing things that are not there."

But theater critics and seasoned artists know that actors are not all-knowing and are unaware that much that is hidden in their unconscious emerges and expresses itself in the course of their acting. In this regard we see some of the shortcomings when theatrical productions about the Bible are performed for the public. Actors who are completely divorced from living the biblical experience will concomitantly be impoverished in their unconscious experiences and their associations will be directed elsewhere. All criticism and exhortations will be of no avail, the actor will not be able to perform what is required of him. Being well versed in the Bible, the sources, and the history of Israel would be a prerequisite, providing the necessary ingredients, thereby enabling the actor to present his role in a different color.

The role of autosuggestion in acting on stage can be seen in the performance of some actors who stutter[25] in daily life but the moment they are on stage, not only do they not stutter but they are able to alter the tone and pitch of their voice in accordance with the role so perfectly that it is hard to believe that they are stutterers.

It is a well known fact that people who stutter when they speak can sing as well as anyone. From this it can be concluded that the stutter is autosuggested, hence deeply embedded in the unconscious. But the moment the stutterer relays across his unconscious mind the idea of singing, that is based upon smooth-tongued functioning and is free of obstructions, he erects a barrier separating all thoughts about compromised tongue and speech, and his singing becomes unconscious and unhampered. Suffice it for the stutterer to create the experience or the image of himself singing, to enable him to speak with fluency like any other person.

All of this is written in order to persuade the reader to try these things on his own and find out that it is neither ridiculous nor irritating but can only be beneficial. All he has to do to is adopt the correct way of thinking by practicing several exercises for a few days and all will be well. It is not enough to read and be satisfied with theoretical knowledge. One has to experiment and do. Only by doing will your efforts bear fruit.

Henry Ford, the practical genius, said that even a genius blessed with many talents will not succeed unless he uses those talents in action. These things are ridiculous in their simplicity, but potential geniuses will recognize the truth in them.

Know what you want to do and do it! And if you do it properly, you will be assured of reaching your goal in the shortest time possible. It is not possible in every instance and in every circumstance to show a person, in advance, how he should organize his thoughts in the proper way in order to have them realized. So we will start with easy things and from them we'll learn the correct pathway leading us to greater and more worthy things.

Most people, upon hearing the chime of the clock without consciously listening to it, will confidently state the number of chimes up to approximately five in number. They can perform more or less the same number of movements without having to count each one of them separately. For example, if a person is asked to take three quick steps without counting each one, we would expect him to be able to accomplish this with ease.

However, if we ask that person to do the same thing and run, say, nine, or a dozen or more steps without counting, he may decline the challenge and many will add that in order to be able to do such a thing one must have a special sense, a unique ability not possessed by mere mortals. And yet, within a few moments, with proper thinking, it turns out that this can be done easily, without any mistakes and without knowing how it was done, just as easily as running two or three steps.

As soon as a person intends doing the more complex action, a thought consisting of the following elements crosses his mind: lack of confidence in his ability to do it and doubt that this can be done at all, including the required motor organization. Given that all of this occurs in the unconscious mind, these are autosuggestions *per se*. And so, the person takes several steps that are not the number required of him and ends up saying, "I don't know," or, "This is unimportant, but had I studied it or been interested in it, or had occupied myself with it, I would probably be able to do things of this nature." Such excuses are offered for many years until the person says instead, "Oh, this is child's play, not fit for someone of my age," and in this way the matter is closed. But we will not be wrong, nor would we exaggerate, if we say that there are many people who are envious of a friend, an acquaintance, or even a stranger, who dances or drums with the tempo and rhythm of any tune.

If we change the numerical composition of the basic elements we mentioned earlier, compositions that differ from person to person, we will also change the outcome. If we create the image of the movement exclusively in our brain, we will in any case inhibit any effort of the will to overcome the lack of confidence and the doubt, thereby allowing the motor idea to materialize with greater intensity and ease. With repeated practice, the internal friction will subside, and the pleasure that comes about consequent to any successful action or physical movement will increase concomitantly.

A stream of satisfying emotional associations will very soon accompany these movements or actions, making them easier and more pleasant to perform. This, in turn, will provide further incentive to want to do and act even more. In other words, this process serves to elevate our vital potential to a higher state.

Let us now see how this is done in a practical way. Take a few steps in a casual and easy manner, both mentally and physically, and say out loud something like this: "I will take precisely seven steps." Say it two or three times. Now visually create an image of yourself taking seven steps without saying anything (you may shut your eyes if you feel it necessary). Now say the word "seven" without thinking about anything else and walk forward. You will probably think it is a coincidence when you count the footprints and see that you walked exactly seven steps.

Try it again and again and you will discover that there is no coincidence in this. Moreover, you may feel while walking that you were unsuccessful on one occasion or another. When that happens, if you pay attention you can discern that a foreign thought or some exertion intruded and hindered you.

Thoughts such as, "I must," or, "I want very much" contain within them the disturbing element of "I can't," or, "This is very difficult." Were it not for these thoughts, you would have been able to fulfill your intention without feeling the internal resistance you are struggling to overcome.

After succeeding several times and it is clear that you will succeed, change the number. You will discover that this time it is easier for you, and you can now do it while muttering the word "seven" under your breath. As you reduce the number of superfluous actions and thoughts and your thinking approaches the same simple and direct situation in which you intended to take two steps and took them, the number of your errors will likewise decrease. Within a few minutes you will be able to walk any number of steps up to fifteen, accurately and with the ease that approaches nonchalance.

The action described is not, in itself, very important, but the way it is done is of great value, one may even say of primary, decisive value because through this process one can achieve a range of actions that were previously unknown, a clear and useful means by which effort will lessen yet output will increase.

Another way of acquiring this system is via the following exercise: hold a pencil and tap it on a piece of paper a certain number of times, let us say six times. Obviously, the aim here is to perform the taps in an automatic manner as if they are occurring on their own, without consciously monitoring them. Also they are to be done so rapidly that counting them is not possible. The manner of doing it is the same as in the previous example. Having done the previous exercise, it will be enough for you to say the word "six" once or twice and at the same time start tapping. (This can be done without looking at the paper.)

Experience demonstrates that in a few minutes it is possible to reach any number of taps with confidence, up to about fifteen, without even the need to count the markings on the paper. All this can be achieved providing the person will say the number out loud and that the action will commence as soon as the word is uttered and that the thought will be singular and isolated.

After doing this many times, and acquiring confidence in your ability, do exactly the same thing except that before starting say out loud: "I very much want to," or, "I'll try," or, "I must not make any mistakes," and start tapping. You will find that the very small number of times you succeed will be by sheer coincidence. This demonstrates that the primary factor in succeeding was not the training, or your desire, but the correct thinking prior to the action.

Proof of this can be seen in the fact that many famous people in the world deteriorate far earlier than their age warrants it. These people, who have been successful because of their effective intuitive thinking, start faltering the moment doubt enters their minds, gnawing at them like moths because they were never aware of how they became so successful in the first place. We can see this most clearly in the world of sport. Suffice it to read about people like Carpentier[26] and Dempsey,[27] accomplished boxers, who upon suffering their first defeat, saw the end of their whole illustrious boxing career.

Bob Fitzsimmons,[28] who appeared in the ring for the last time at age forty-seven, is proof that age was not the contributing factor. With the others it was as if the rug had been pulled out from under their feet. Their thread of thought was severed and no amount of effort could reconnect it. This is what happens to people who lose control of their natural resources of strength and ability, God-given treasures that are the envy of man.

Now for the last exercise: place a target in front of you, or simply draw a circle with a radius of about ten centimeters (four inches) and try to hit it by throwing a ball or a smooth stone at it. Increase the throwing distance until you fail to hit the target ten out of ten throws.

This being the third exercise, it would be worthwhile, for the sake of proof, to further simplify the principle of performing the culmination of the action correctly: take the ball in your hand, do not say or murmur anything. With closed eyes, imagine the target in front of you and in your imagination throw the ball and hit the target. At the exact moment that you see the ball striking the target in your mind's eye, open your eyes, locate the target and throw the ball at it.

The time interval between seeing the target and throwing the ball must be as short as possible. If you try this after doing the previous exercises, you will immediately feel whether you can succeed or not. Correct whatever is necessary and now you will hit the target with every throw. It is not important to clarify this whole process, i.e., to repeat everything we have already described. However, it is worthwhile noting that shortening the time between seeing the target and throwing the ball reduces the possibility of other thoughts interjecting themselves, apart from that of the ball hitting the target. This, together with eliminating the application of willpower, allows the thought of hitting the ball to reach its goal undisturbed, thereby simplifying, facilitating, and accelerating the achievement of the primary thought.

On their own, these are not very important things and may even seem insignificant to experienced people, although they may be interesting as games for children. It is true that the exercises *per se* are not of the greatest importance and do not constitute the major portion of this system, but the way they are carried out is of paramount importance. If it is possible, simply by thinking, to direct a ball to go in the intended direction without having trained yourself to do so, you will have benefited enormously and will have grasped an important principle, one that to date you have not used but will help you in the future. You will be holding a tool in your hands that will help you to perform any task with ease and precision.

If you are an accountant, you will expand your range of absorbing and understanding matters in your field. You will learn to swim, to ride a bicycle, to dance to the rhythm of music, to engage in any sport, any activity you may be interested in, be it abstract knowledge, spiritual, or material. You can learn these things. It will serve you in all of these. It will be pleasant to do anything you wish to do because there will be no accompanying effort or strain.

The beginning may be difficult and frustrating but you will end up having gained much. It may seem ridiculous to you, to pamper yourself and you may not want people to think of you as Eli the High Priest[29] thought of Hannah[30] the mother of Samuel. Or perhaps in so doing, your self esteem will be diminished? In some respect you would be right; ironically, anyone learning in maturity seems a little odd, and yet those who study in their maturity learn more than in their childhood. And this is only the beginning; as you proceed you will forget how you came about this in the first place. Rabbi Akiva[31] himself, who was middle-aged when he started to study, was probably the object of ridicule.

Einstein, too, labored and studied until he understood the meaning of the numeral "one." Can we compare their final accomplishments to their modest beginnings? It is no exaggeration to claim that it is possible for every person to rise to such heights by using this method, and even if it seems unrealistic, the truth is that anyone can attain more, much more, by using this method, than he can without using it.

There are those who say: "Nothing can stand in the way of willpower,"[32] but every person knows that there are many things standing in their way. Who has not experienced the taste of an irritating thought pestering him and returning just as fast as he brushes it away? Who is not aware that we cannot eradicate a thought by directly struggling with it because the thought wins?

Only by going indirectly, around and about, and by using different thoughts, can we overcome it. Willpower is the force we apply to coerce this or that thought to linger in our brain, but this is not the force that rules. Control resides in imagination and in correct thinking.

Biography[33, 34]

Moshe Feldenkrais, D.Sc., (1904 – 1984)

Moshe Feldenkrais, D.Sc.
(1904-1984). Photo courtesy of
Feldenkrais Institute Tel Aviv, Israel.

The *Feldenkrais Method* was developed by Dr. Moshe Feldenkrais (1904 – 1984).

Moshe Feldenkrais (Doctor of Science, Sorbonne) was an engineer, physicist, inventor, martial artist, and student of human development. Born in Slavuta, present-day Ukraine, to a distinguished family known as high-quality publishers of Jewish publications, he emigrated as a Zionist at age fourteen to Palestine where he worked as a laborer, studied martial arts, and completed his high school at age twenty-three—with honors. After working as a cartographer for the British survey office, he left for France where he graduated in 1933 from the Ècole de

25

Traveaux Publics de Paris in Mechanical and Electrical Engineering. Later, he studied at the Sorbonne while working under Frederic Joliot-Curie at the Radium Institute in Paris. His interest in Jiu-Jitsu brought him into contact with Professor Jigaro Kano, who developed Judo. Dr. Feldenkrais was a founder of the Jiu-Jitsu Club of Paris and was one of the first Europeans to earn a black belt in Judo (1936).

Escaping the Nazi advance he went to Britain and worked on anti-submarine research for the British Admiralty. It was there, in the forties, motivated by his attempts to heal a recurring knee injury first sustained while playing soccer in 1929 and uncertain prospects for surgery, that he began to develop his Method and wrote his first book on the subject. Thus began for Feldenkrais a life-long exploration of the relationship between movement and consciousness. In the fifties, Dr. Feldenkrais returned to Israel where he lived and taught his method that has now spread across the globe. He died in 1984 in Tel Aviv, Israel.

In developing his work, Moshe Feldenkrais studied, among other things, anatomy, physiology, child development, movement science, evolution, psychology, and a number of Eastern awareness practices and other somatic approaches.

Dr. Feldenkrais authored a number of seminal books on movement, learning, human consciousness, and somatic experience. He taught in Israel and many countries in Europe through the sixties and seventies and in North America through the seventies and eighties. He trained his first group of teachers in Tel Aviv in the early seventies. This was followed by two groups in the USA— one group in San Francisco, California and another in Amherst, Massachusetts.

In his life Dr. Feldenkrais worked with and helped tens of thousands of people with functional movement disorders. The focus of his work was using movement and the accompanying sensation of movement as the vehicle by which his students learned and perfected their functional abilities, hence he called his work Awareness through Movement. By providing an enormous range of learning experiences to people of all ages and disabilities, he freed them from restrictions imposed by static medical diagnoses. He helped heads of state such as David ben Gurion and Moshe Dayan, artists such as Yehudi Menhuhin, sports figures such as Dr. J., children with cerebral palsy, and countless others.

He taught over a number of years for the dramatist Peter Brook and his Théâtre Bouffes du Nord. He was a collaborator with thinkers such as anthropologist Margaret Mead, neuroscientist Karl Pribram, and explorers of the psychophysical Jean Houston and Robert Masters.

The breadth, vitality, and precision of Dr. Feldenkrais's work has seen it applied in fields as diverse as neurology, psychology, performing arts, sports, and rehabilitation.

Endnotes

1. *The Practice of Autosuggestion, by the method of Émile Coué*, by C. Harry Brooks is available free online: www.gutenberg.org/files/29339-h/29339-h.htm.

2. Clyde Kluckhohn, author of *Mirror for Man*, McGraw Hill, NY 1965, pp. 135, 136.

3. School still extant under the title: Society of Applied Psychology.

4. Charles Baudouin, 1893 – 1963. Coué's student and Practical Psychoanalyst, author of: *Suggestion and Autosuggestion*. Free e-book.

5. Henri-Louis Bergson 1859 – 1941. French Philosopher, author of *Introduction to Metaphysics*.

6. William James, 1842 – 1910. Proponent of Functionalism in Psychology. Author of *Principles of Psychology* and of the James-Lange theory of emotion.

7. In a recent telephone conversation with Professor Shulamit Kreitler, she stated that at that period she was a lecturer in the Department of Psychology at Tel Aviv University.

8. T. X. Barber, not T. K. Typo in original text. Theodore X. Barber, *Hypnosis: A Scientific Approach*, Van Nostrand Reinhold, 1969.

9. "Meanings, culture and communication," Original Research Article, *Journal of Pragmatics, Volume 12, Issues 5-6, December 1988, Pages 725-742*, Shulamith Kreitler, Hans Kreitler.

10. "Sof ma'aseh bemachshavah techilah" means "Last in deed, first in thought," i.e., the final outcome has been conceived at the outset (or, in current usage: there is no value in doing something unless it is preceded by thought and intention). It indicates that while the Sabbath was the last event in the story of creation it was first in thought. The source is from "Lecha Dodi Likrat Kala", a liturgical song composed by Rabbi Shlomo Halevi Alkabetz, a

16th century Kabbalist from Safed. It is sung in the home or in the synagogue on Fridays at dusk, welcoming the Sabbath as one would welcome a bride.

11. Moshe Feldenkrais: We have to differentiate between the will of the person wanting to jump off a dangerous high point into a deep ditch and the desire to jump by a person confident in his ability to do so. The first is deterred by the great internal resistance accompanying him, but in the second, on the contrary, it assists the jump, since the pleasure of the movements and the competitive uplifting of the spirit emerge subsequent to the act itself.

12. "TaNaKh"—Acronym for the three major portions of the Bible: Torah: the five books of Moses or the Pentateuch, Nevi'im: the Prophets, Ktuvim: the Writings.

13. Yonah Girundi, 1210 – 1263. Of the same generation as Maimonedes, the "Rambam" (Rabbi Moshe ben Maimon) in Spain.

14. Rabbi Moshe Ben Nachman, 1195 – 1270, also known as Nachmanides. He was Rabbi Yonah's cousin. He participated in a disputation (theological argument with the Catholic Church) in Barcelona in 1263. Although he won, he was forced to flee Spain, and as a result, all future disputations forbade the Jewish participants to answer frankly. At age seventy-two he settled in Jerusalem, reorganized the Jewish community and moved to Acre (Akko), to become the head of its Jewish community.

15. A small portion of it. In it he also instructs his son to read the letter weekly.

16. Rabbi Sa'adia Gaon, 882 – 942 CE. The greatest of the Geonim (geniuses) of the Talmudic era in Sura, Babylon.

17. Rabbi Eliezer ben Horkanus was one of the great teachers of the Mishna—(1st century CE). According to Jewish tradition, God gave both the Written Law (Torah) and the Oral Law to Moses on Mount Sinai. For centuries, only the Torah appeared as a written text. Following the destruction of the Jewish community and its Temple in Jerusalem by the Romans, and fearing that the oral traditions might be forgotten, Judah HaNassi (circa 200 CE) undertook the mission of compiling them in what became known as the Mishna. The Mishna consists of 63 tractates codifying Jewish laws, which are the basis of the Talmud (studies, debates, discussion of those laws.

18. Paavo Nurmi, aka the Flying Finn 1897 – 1973. During the 1920s he was the best middle and long distance runner in the world.

19. In our times it would be Muhammad Ali, the boxer.

20. Sir Robert Baden-Powell, 1857 – 1941, founder of the Boy Scouts movement.

21. Eustace Hamilton Miles, 1868 – 1948. He won an Olympic silver medal at age thirty-nine.

22. Moshe Feldenkrais: Indeed, we have here an incomplete explanation. The purpose of proper breathing during exercise is not only to have a healthy exchange of air, but also to open the air channels to the extent that they can supply the body with all of its needs in any situation and in the worst conditions too. Proper breathing should be second nature to the person, hence it is important for the person to gradually stop paying attention to his breathing while exercising, of course only after acquiring and habituating himself to comfortable and hygienic breathing. Exaggerating its importance and ruminating about it is an unfortunate habit from which one has to be weaned.

23. Feodor Chaliapin, 1873 – 1938, the great Russian opera singer.

24. Savva Mamontov, 1841 – 1918, a prominent Russian business-man who became a patron of Russian opera and was responsible for the discovery of the unique talent of Feodor Chaliapin.

25. Israeli audiences know this. One of their favorite actors stutters.

26. Georges Carpentier, 1894 – 1975, French light heavyweight world champion. He lost his fight with Jack Dempsey in the heavyweight division, July, 1921.

27. Jack Dempsey, 1895 – 1983, American heavyweight champion. He lost his title to Gene Tunney.

28. Bob Fitzsimmons, 1863 – 1917. He was the first triple weight division world champion, claiming his third, the light heavyweight title, at age forty-one.

29. Eli was the priest (Cohen) during the time the Tabernacle was still in Shiloh, prior to the construction of the First Temple in Jerusalem.

30. Hannah was one of seven women to whom God gave the power of prophesy. Hannah was barren for many years. Finally, on one of the festive Holidays, she went to the tabernacle to pray and plead for a child. Upon seeing her, Eli, the priest rebuked her, thinking that she was drunk. She calmly responded that she was not drunk but was in great sorrow, praying for a child. Eli blessed her so that her prayers would be answered. She soon gave birth to Samuel, who became one of the greatest leaders of the Jewish people, known as Samuel the prophet, and known for appointing the first Jewish kings, Saul and David.

31. Rabbi Akiva, 50 – 135 CE. He joined the fight against the Romans who subsequently destroyed Jerusalem. He was a poor, uneducated shepherd who began studying Torah as an adult. He became a great scholar and teacher, and is considered one of the greatest rabbis of all time.

Endnotes

32. Current usage: Where there is a will, there is a way.

33. Mark Reese, 1951 – 2006. Author of *Moshe Feldenkrais - A Life in Movement, Volume 1*.

34. IFF Materials Website. *Moshe Feldenkrais Biography*, http://feldenkrais-method.org/en/biography.

Resources

For information about the *Feldenkrais Method* Books, CDs, Downloads,
DVDs, articles and other resources, contact:

The *Feldenkrais* Store
P.O. Box 2615, Longmont, CO 80502.
www.AchievingExcellence.com

For information about Moti Nativ and Warrior Awareness,
visit www.Warriors-Awareness.com

For information about *Feldenkrais Method* practitioners and
professional trainings, contact:

The *Feldenkrais* Guild of North America
5436 N. Albina Ave, Portland, OR 97217.
www.Feldenkrais.com

The Israeli *Feldenkrais* Guild
PO Box 3025, TelAviv 6,103,001.
www.Feldenkrais-Israel.org